A Walking Friendship: The First 500 Miles

As a two-time Appalachian Trail thru-hiker, competitive triathlete, long distance kayaker and all around "busy" person, *A Walking Friendship* was an invitation for me to slow down, breathe, and notice. This gentle book honors the many ways we can be present in nature and with each other. Diane's and Carole's writing is humble and heartfelt—and the photography, breathtaking. It is all there in plain sight, for an appreciative eye and a willing heart.

Joanna Ezinga

The whole of *A Walking Friendship: The First 500 Miles* feels like a guided meditation. And it is. A guided retrospective meditation through woods and ponds and streams and paths. A guided retrospective meditation through blossoming friendship. A guided retrospective meditation through self-awareness and mindfulness.

Using poems, photographs and prose, it offers the reader richness and pause: a richness to savor, and pause for time to meditate on one's own journeys, friendships, and relationships.

It offers the reader humor as well as challenges, and a look at intimate relationships between self and friend; self and self; and self and nature. I couldn't put it down, but I know I will go back to it again and again.

Cynthia Brackett-Vincent, *publisher and editor,*
The Aurorean: New England's Premier Independent Poetry Journal

Diane and Carole have undertaken to bring to the reader a mixed media experience. Despite the risk involved in such an attempt, they take us with them as they meander through some of nature's most exquisite sights and sounds. The simplicity of it carries the reader along. We share the wondering and wandering.

Here is a nature dessert that you plan on taking only a bite of, and can't help but consume in one sitting. Then you go back and read again, to savor the wisdom and glory of it all.

Dr. Gladys Craig, *Associate Professor of English Emerita, Sage Colleges*

A WALKING FRIENDSHIP

the first 500 miles

DIANE KAVANAUGH-BLACK *and* CAROLE FULTS

A Walking Friendship: The First 500 Miles
Copyright © 2020 by Diane Kavanaugh-Black & Carole Fults, and Sea-Lily Publications

BOOK DESIGN BY The Troy Book Makers

ISBN: 978-1-61468-602-6

Previous Publication Information

Earlier versions of Diane's "Lions and Tigers and Peaches, Oh My!," "The Day of Slow-Moving Bees," "The Journey Back from Hidden Pond," "January Thaw," "Surprises on the Path," "The Poet in the Woods," and "Landing: A Tale of Very Late Spring," along with accompanying photos by Diane, appeared on the website www.OfTheEssenceBlog.com.

Diane's photo "Partridge Run Sign," as well as "Joe Pye Weed (Eutrochium) Against Evergreens," and "Edges over Ice Crystals" were part of our shared photo show "Pickerel Ponds" at Bethlehem Public Library, Delmar, NY, December 2015.

Diane's "Acorn Cap in Ice" was exhibited at the Emily Treadwell Thacher Nature Photography Show, March 2016 and "Pheasant Feather Caught By a Leaf," March 2018.

Carole's poems *Sprites, Fishing, Mid-Summer, Cries of Wild Things, 4 Ponds and a Bog, The Story of the Watcher at Wood Duck Pond, Mountain Lake with Crows, Proof of Wind, I Walk the Labyrinth,* and *Today I Came Looking* were published in her book *All the World is an Asana* (2016). Her poem *Vernal Ponds* was also published in the Spring/Summer Issue of *The Aurorean: New England's Premier Independent Poetry Journal. Walk the Labyrinth* was previously published in *Sister My Sister: An Anthology of Sisterhood* (Starshine Publishing, Boulder CO, November 2015). Her poetry is also available on her blog at www.carolefults.com.

Carole's photo "Reflective Rock at 9 Corner Lake" was shown at an exhibit at Zion Lutheran Church, Schenectady NY, in November 2014. Her "Dragonfly" photo was exhibited at "Pickerel Ponds" at the Bethlehem Public Library, December 2015 and at the Emily Treadwell Thacher Nature Photography Show, March 2016.

Maps used by permission of the New York State Department of Environmental Conservation.

Dedicated to the forest
and all the more-than-human ones who live there.

May our efforts here help
the preservation of our shared home.

And with gratitude to Diane.

— CAROLE

We offer this book in the hope that readers might discover
some of the joy, peace and relationship we find in the
practice of wandering and exploring the outdoors.

Thanks to Carole, for her patient presence
and sense of adventure and humor.

Thanks to all of the guides in our lives.

— DIANE

AUTHORS' NOTE

Any errors in plant or animal identification, habitat facts, etcetera, are completely our own.

Although we enjoy researching what we find in the wild (or in the city for that matter), we are not scientists, botanists or animal behaviorists. We are absolutely aware we could be totally wrong about anything and everything.

TABLE OF CONTENTS

Poems and essays are indicated in bold
and photos/images in standard print.

Attribution of photography:
CAF for Carole Fults, DKB for Diane Kavanaugh-Black.

A PREFACE PROSE POEM
by Diane and Carole

Let's be clear.

We the authors,
Carole and Diane,
are not Adirondack 46ers,
members of the Catskill 3500 Club,
or goal driven, long distance
Appalachian Trail hikers.

Pokey.
That's us.

We stop to take photos, catch breath
notice bugs and bark and dirt,
squawking, rustlings, and quiet,
honeysuckle's sweetness,
the stench of dead deer,
flow
or not
of water,
how the rocks listen
and mark our footsteps.

We think. We write. We talk a little,

walk a little.

Listen and look.

Breathe

in and out.

Walk again.

From day to day

hour to hour,

a path is never the same.

Seasons glide or stumble in.

So do we.

Pokey, we are.

Sometimes

these bodies hurt.

Unsure joints, tight muscles

limp along.

Sometimes

these hearts hurt

with the unsure in our lives

tightness and pain in the world

quick shots of injury

long-lived-with decay.

Sometimes
we chatter
like our friends the squirrels.
Sometimes
tears hang
on the corners of our eyes
like dew on strawberry leaves
lush to the ground.

Sometimes
we cry out in frustration
the crows and blue jays above
also indignant.

Sometimes
sometimes
we are quiet,
lean comfortable
into our slowness,
look
into the green
or gold
or nakedness
of the trees,
and what hurts
doesn't ache
quite so much.

Partridge Run Wildlife Management Area

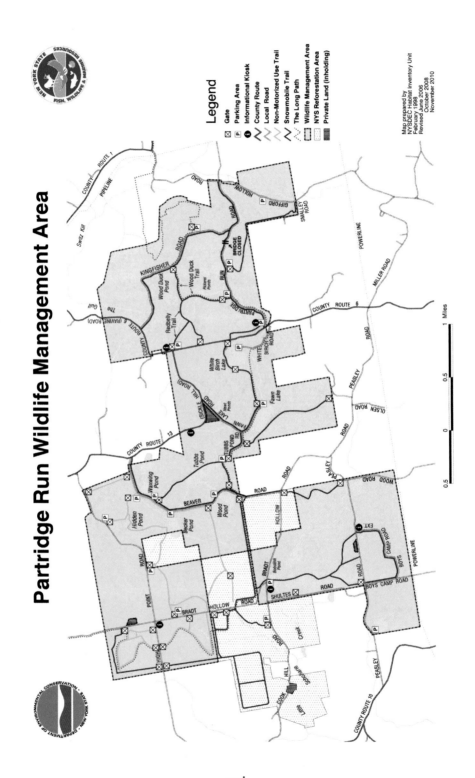

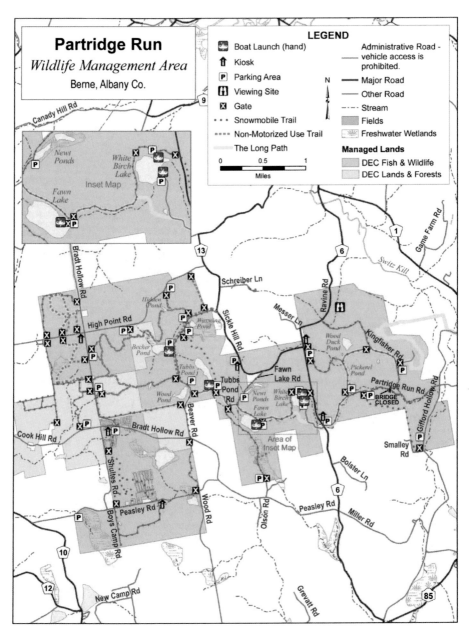

*Maps used by permission of the New York State Department
of Environmental Conservation.*

Reflective Rock at 9 Corner Lake (CAF)

THE VERY BEGINNING

It's March, 2012. Carole confidently drives her red SUV north and west; we are on a trip from Albany, New York to explore the southern Adirondacks. Originally a group outing, the day trip has dwindled to two participants—Carole and me. Though we are in a writing group together, we don't really know each other very well.

On the way, I study the tourist brochures she'd gathered and we agree on a couple options: the Good Luck Cliffs and Jockeybush Lake. Some nicely overstuffed sandwiches are tucked in her backpack, and I've brought orange sections. After two hours, plus a stop at a tiny grocery for dessert sweets, we arrive.

A creek has washed out the first path. We try another, and the paint blazes on trees that mark the trail fade to nothing. It doesn't upset us because along the way we admire and take pictures of beautiful views along the curvy cliff edge. We joke about the not-just-crabby but hostile woman at the store: "Cookies? You want cookies? What the hell for?" (We ended up buying the $8 bag of Oreos, anyway.) As we crunch our chocolate treats, we problem solve about poison ivy avoidance and map interpretation.

At the end, we are fully sated and perfectly happy for not having finished any of the planned routes.

On the Thruway, on our way back from that first foray, Carole darts her eyes hesitantly at me, then back to the highway.

"Since I retired, I've been wanting to walk more regularly. Do you think you might want to do that?" A pause. "I have these places I want to explore, and you have time during the week, like me…."

At this moment, I am two years out from a move across the country and concurrent career interruption, followed immediately by a completely unexpected divorce, exhausting illness and major surgery. I am slowly recovering as I settle into this new life and figure out my next job—and my internal life.

My brain scrambles silently in response to her question. What if I am too weak from my surgery to keep up? Will she be mad if I try it and don't like it? Today was fun, but what kind of person will she be to hike with long term? What am I committing to, exactly?

Then again, I think, her offer is not pushy. She's just asked: Want to try this? I feel the sweetness of the invitation, since we've talked on this day about my painful life changes and struggles with workaholic perfectionism, and especially about how I spend my time. I leap in, leaving any questions to be resolved later.

"Sure, I would like to walk more, too."

I settle back in my seat. In a new spirit of experimentation, I decide that I am fine if we walk a couple times and then are done; I will enjoy whatever we do, no expectations.

It is a slow start. Four months later we finally get together again, this time to explore a seasonal Adirondack road, the Powley-Piseco. We ooh and ahh over boulder-filled streams. The water leads our eyes to more distant dabs of dark brown hemlock and whitish pink paper birch, and then the cornflower blue sky. After Carole drives us to the end of the rough gravel road and then east on 29A, we stop again. From the pull off, we hike the typically Adirondack, rooty and rocky mile to Nine Corner Lake.

After scrambling through bushes to get the best camera angle on the still water, I laugh out loud. "Hiking together is really fun!"

Carole squats slowly to examine curls of floating acorns and pine needles. Her knees crack on the way down and then on the way up. "I agree, but the drive plus the walking is a bit much. Let's find some closer places to wander."

Our focus shifts to the natural world south of Albany. We pick one day a week to meet, depending on weather and health and outside obligations. The patterns established that first hike continue: Carole transports us in her sturdy four-wheel-drive vehicle and I bring maps. We experience plentiful tasty food, funny stories, uncertain pathways, and always, always — kindness and gentleness with each other.

How could I know that spring invitation back in 2012 would begin years of weekly walks and hikes, years of quiet conversation and snacks we delight in? That it would begin a deep friendship, a creative relationship, and the discovery of a long-latent naturalist within me?

Who knew?

That's the point, I realize, looking back: some people follow an inclination (Carole) and others an invitation (me) to see where it leads them. You don't know what it will bring, on a path or in your life. It could be awful—it could be wondrous and life-changing—or it could be both.

Clover and Bird's-foot Trefoil (DKB)

PARTRIDGE RUN:
A Further Invitation and Beginning

SOON IT'S EARLY AUGUST 2013. Carole and I have been taking nature walks together for over a year.

Carole says, "I went to this place called Partridge Run a decade ago, and I want to get to know it better. It seems really interesting, but I don't want to go by myself. Especially since it's a Wildlife Management Area, so sometimes there are hunters."

We get two maps from the internet. On our first trip there, we bumble our way around the local roads, half-lost, and find a couple of trailheads. It does not look promising: an overgrown road, with mosquitoes that attack us as we get out of the car.

Once we start, however, the trail called Partridge Run Road leads us alongside a flat stone ledge and stream, with a trickling waterfall below. Pines lean over us and the path sometimes breaks open into sunny meadows. Four-foot-tall burdock borders the woods: burdock with its large leaves like rhubarb and thin flower stalks sporting deep purple at the tips of prickly burrs.

We spy some startlingly tall, rosy-headed plants. "Oh, milkweed!" I enthuse. Carole makes a face. "I don't think this is milkweed; the leaves look wrong."

Research after the hike—another pattern started—proves the fluffs of pale pink are known as Joe-Pye weed, and are part of a plant genus in the sunflower family called *Eutrochium*. (The group also includes white boneset, a plant I had heard of before but never seen.) Behind the Joe-Pye weed, I glimpse my first hummingbird in its natural habitat. Grayish, it buzzes to my left and then over toward cattail-edged Pickerel Ponds.

*A later visit to the waterfall off **Partridge Run Road*** (CAF)

The air and light have definitely shifted toward fall, Carole and I agree, and the wildflowers, too. Last year's shotgun shells and other bullet casings dot the ground, half-buried in the mounds of white and purple and yellow blossoms. They remind us, if we return, to start wearing bright orange on our heads and backs come October.

The second trip, we choose Tubbs Pond from the map as our destination. On the way, the mosquitoes continue to make us miserable as they bite and tickle our sweaty faces. Sunblock melts into our eyes as we pant up and down the hills. We see frogs jump out of the woods path and plonk into puddles. A turkey vulture and red-tailed hawk circle together as we start up the Long Path. The moving-into-fall flowers glory in the sun: goldenrod and buttercup, bee balm and New England asters, black-eyed Susans and white daisies and milkweed pods and fields of now familiar Joe-Pye weed. The rainbow of blooms attracts a huge tiger swallowtail butterfly, another nature walk first for me.

When we go off into the trees near Tubbs Pond, Carole whispers, "Oh this is a fairytale woods! A storybook woods!"

She is right: the tall red pines make for deep and dark stillness. Inside, a hill of dirt, rock and tree roots rises. At eye level the pines' thick rusty plates of bark curve up to huge limbs and then sprays of silent two-needled bunches. The canopy overhead shadows and cools us, snuggled-in, so different from the bright sunshine out at the pond. After we enter, we hear no planes or boats or people, just the movement of treetops in the wind, our own feet and jostling packs, and the low buzz of insects, all of which slow, soften and stop inside the forest. Even the large black-and-blue-winged dragonflies make no noise. Anything could happen here: real dragons, maybe a giant beanstalk.

*Joe-Pye weed (**Eutrochium**) against evergreens, Pickerel Ponds* (DKB)

Carole that day in the Fairytale Woods (DKB)

I know I am with the right person when Carole throws herself down on her back at the base of a three-story tall evergreen, needles and dust be damned, to get just the right angle through her camera lens.

With that action, she teaches me to approach our hikes ready to get silly and muddy, with a child's wonder, and with open eyes and ears and heart.

Over years to come, that openness continues to resonate, not only at Tubbs Pond but all the ponds and watercourses at Partridge Run, along with the snowmobile paths and administrative roads and Long Path trails. It resonates with the squawk of blue jays near the fairytale woods, with whispers of water lapping the dock at Tubbs, and the crunch of my hiking boots on gravel, sand, dirt and stone; later on snow and ice. We get to know ourselves and investigate our own changing seasons in this place. Truths emerge. We yearn to return again and again—and we do.

Tree Man lives by Hidden Pond (CAF)

SPRITES

Just beyond the edge of hearing and seeing
a blanket of Spirit wraps round the pine forest
where live and pray the sprites
making rituals
in the sunlight
on the pine needle floor.

Wind, like ocean waves in tree tops,
in these white pines
always a special mood,
a particular atmosphere —
sounds, lights, air
anticipating
the presence of a familiar.

FISHING

On solstice
the Blue Heron in its pond
moves slowly, deliberately
or stands in silence undisturbed.

Graceful, accurate
it spears a fish
and returns to stillness.

The Heron (CAF)

Red Eft, the terrestrial stage of Eastern newts (DKB)

LIONS AND TIGERS
AND PEACHES, OH MY!

ONE LATE AUGUST MORNING early in our adventures, Carole and I hike an overgrown path off High Point Road. Like two girls in a fairy tale, we hop and skip and lollygag, cameras instead of baskets-to-Grandma in hand. Small frogs surprise, bursting up with powerful rear legs from well-hidden spots in the mud. Red efts appear and disappear, foreshortened limbs squiggling their torsos in cartoon fashion.

We mosey along, but then are stopped short by poison ivy thickly encroaching the whole route. Smartly, we turn around.

"Better safe than sorry," Carole quips, and I agree.

On the trail back to the car, we spy something. A dark thing, in the middle of the path. A rock? A tree limb? An ailing creature?

Cue the scary Little Red Riding Hood music.

I kneel down to examine it. Look up at my hiking partner, concerned. Look down to take in the evidence again. Squint up as we nod simultaneously.

"Yup."

"Looks like it."

"Bear scat, huh?"

"See the blackberry seeds in it?"

"It smells musky around here–must be pretty fresh."

"Oh. Here in the mud. A claw print."

Straightaway, we realize we should have been alert in the woods for something other than late summer wildflowers, amphibians, and butterflies.

15

We quickly reorient to the aqua paint on the trees—Long Path "blazes" that mark our exit out.

Only once before I'd been close to a bear in the wild (and known it), and that was a few months earlier at Kripalu, the yoga center in Massachusetts. One early morning as the sangha gathered around the teacher, he noted dryly: "You may want to look out the window."

Across the back lawn, a youngster *Ursidae* was galumphing and gamboling, presumably drawn by the smell of our breakfast cooking. Since we saw the bear through glass, it was much more like a zoo encounter than a live one, though it made us all think twice before taking the paths alone at dusk.

Bears have also shown up in my nightmares. Terror comes from a sudden smothering attack in the dark, from the inability to escape a creature so much larger and more powerful than me.

Awake, what I do know about bears is this: black bears live in this part of New York, but not brown bears or the subset of brown bears known as grizzlies, which have a reputation for being more aggressive than black bears. The advice: Don't hang out near rich food sources like wild raspberry bushes. Don't get between a mother bear and her cubs. Hibernation starts in October, and if you see a bear in January be very careful: it is likely a female, in labor, the most inclined to attack.

On the other hand, I have heard many stories of fairly peaceable bear-human encounters where everybody just backed away. Except when conditioned to find food in campsites, bird feeders and garbage cans, bears are reclusive. Some hikers proactively announce their presence by making noise, shaking bells or singing.

Which, back in the woods, we proceed to do.

Helpful Carole begins to shout.

"Oh Mr. Bear, Mr. Bear… SHE'S the plump and juicy one. I am the old stringy one." She pauses, as if listening. "Yes, the one with the baseball cap, that's her."

Only half-laughing, we speed our legs to cover territory fast, then faster.

She continues: "Oh Mr. Bear, Mr. Bear! We had a lovely visit, but we're leaving now!"

Arriving unscathed at the car, we aren't ready to give up on our day in spite of run-ins with poison ivy and bear poo. We drive south, arriving at a more civilized path, one that leads to Tubbs Pond.

I remark as we sit down by the water, "Glad I didn't stop to eat my lunch in the woods."

Then it dawns on me the horrendous portent of what I carried in my bag, into what had proven to be active bear territory—cue more sinister music—as Carole hollers gleefully into the trees nearby:

"Oh Mr. Bear! Mr. Bear! She's got A QUARTER OF A PEACH PIE in her bag!"

I whisper, with more dawning, in fact a veritable sunburn of realization, "And a sandwich, peanut butter and–"

Whereupon Carole adds with relish to her public service announcement: "AND HONEY!"

Peach pie at Tubbs Pond (DKB)

In the sunlight of the Tubbs Pond dock, safely consuming my late-summer pastry, I think: *Huh.* In our hurry to get the heck outta there, fresh bear scat in our noses, I had not stopped to take pictures. And am beginning to regret it.

I venture to Carole: "Can we go back? I'd love to get a picture maybe of the tracks…is that crazy?"

After I ask, my heart thumps in my throat like our legs had moved earlier: a little fast, then faster. Without too much hesitation, she acquiesces.

"I guess it would only be twenty minutes to walk back. But shouldn't we be scared?"

Of course I am afraid. It will be a calculated risk. End of summer, blackberries obviously nearby, recent proof right in our footsteps of large alarming creatures–at least one of them. But if I let the fear beat me, I might regret it forever. Plus I really want photographic evidence of what we'd seen.

Lately, I'd felt tired of being afraid of things, always stopping with "Maybe I'll hurt myself. Maybe I'll look stupid. Maybe this is a bad idea."

My new more honest self replies, "Of course maybe I'll hurt myself doing new things, and of course I look stupid sometimes, and yes, maybe the bear will return to the scene of its crime—er, droppings,"—but should I let that keep me away?

My pulse continues to quicken. I note and then ignore it as we climb back into Carole's vehicle. After all, it is with some knowledge that we are deciding to proceed—to make noise, and look up and around while hiking, not just at our feet. Aware that if the wind is blowing at your back, the bear can smell you up to a mile away; if at your face, you can stumble on them, because they can't smell you at all.

Not out of the car a minute, hand cupped around her mouth, my buddy starts.

"The peach pie is in her belly, if you're looking for a treat."

Jingling keys and singing, we find the path. She mumbles under her breath.

"Can't believe we are going back into bear infested woods to get a rat-sa-fratsa picture."

I think to myself that if I get attacked by a bear, I'm gonna not only feel stupid, I'm going to have BEEN stupid.

Off to the side, something dark and thick swims forward in the woods. My eyes bulge and attention narrows sharply. "Oh my god, there's a bear!"

"–Oh, a burned stump." In pseudo bravery, an aside to the cutthroat hiking partner: "Here is where in the scary movie they say: Don't do it! Don't go back! You know there are bears in there!" Heart still banging hard, I slow my inhale, slow my exhale.

It doesn't help.

Maybe this IS a scary movie, I think. Maybe I AM part of a fairy tale, but I can't ponder that now; I'm busy paying attention to my surroundings. I shake my keys louder. We walk quickly, one ahead, one in back.

"I will stay behind you and have my camera ready, so I can take pictures when the bear comes out to greet you," Carole snickers mercilessly.

I hope she knows it's OK to take pictures with a small camera, but not one with a big lens, because the bear interprets that as a large and very aggressive eye. I do know that when you encounter a bear, you look sideways at the ground, and back away or circle around.

We arrive at the fated spot much more quickly than we thought we would; fear definitely distorts your sense of time. Involved in looking for the prints again, we walk along the path identifying deer and raccoon in the thick mud, and others, including the horses' hooves we'd seen all over Partridge Run.

Scat (DKB)

Then there they are–round, small, but bear's prints, definitely not dog, definitely not people or coyote…click-click goes the camera. I neglect to check the woods every second or two. In fact, the more bear-free minutes that pass, the less afraid I feel. We finish and hurry back to the car, the distance even shorter this time.

On our final steps: "A granola bar, Mr. Bear, I think she's got one of THOSE still."

I am glad I have a hiking partner who was willing to go back, even if she was (verbally anyway) also willing to throw me to the omnivores. Glad I got to enjoy my peach pie, and the fairy tale lesson did not involve being swallowed and cut out again, or some outside hero saving me. Glad I've learned to not live without fear but to feel it and choose my action.

Having a wicked-funny friend along sure helps.

(Because the dung was small, I chose to think it was a younger, smaller bear. Not necessarily true, according to my scientist friends. Oh my. The claw prints were in pebbly and wet mud, making the images hard to interpret, or even identify as prints at all.)

THE RIVER

Sitting by this river,
facing downstream,
facing upstream.
God's breath flows over the waters
moving the currents,
flooding the shores of my heart
with joy,
with love
for the magic of the shining wetness
and the kiss of Spirit
that gives us life.

Golden Field (CAF)

MID-SUMMER

Mid-summer leaf shed
water droplets shimmer on a fallen leaf
and a crow calls across the blue, blue emptiness.
There is a half-moon sitting in the morning sky.

Give me a shaded trail in the hotness of summer
where the moon, a crow, a deer, butterflies and mosquitoes
cross my path as if by accident,
a Blue Jay feather falls on my foot as if by chance,
and blissful gratitude the only valid response.

Pheasant feather caught by a leaf (DKB)

LEAF AND FEATHER

Falling leaves and floating feathers
light and effortless on a summer wind
traveling, tumbling past my vision,
held by ever changing airy currents
easily and gently.
No map
no destination
no names
just leaf and feather
flying above an overgrown meadow
where dandelion fuzz drifts up to travel with them,
all seeking the circulating winds.

Searching bee on goldenrod (DKB)

THE DAY OF SLOW-
MOVING BEES

THE MORNING OF AUGUST 15 is cooler in the Helderbergs than it has been in months, only in the mid-50s by 10 a.m. Bees at Newt Pond cling to the goldenrod, languid movie stars on incandescent chaise lounges. After the drama of previous weeks' nectar gathering and pollen dispersing, they barely crawl around: aware they have scenes to perform, but disinclined to rise just yet.

It is The Day of Slow-Moving Bees.

A beaten down path through thigh-high wild bergamot, knapweed, and Queen Anne's lace leads us to the dock on Tubbs Pond. Carole and I are slow-moving bees ourselves as we drive from pond to pond instead of walking, only gradually warming our muscles. The yellowing of trees across the water becomes obvious as we sit with tuna sandwiches, garden tomatoes, and a huge tub of cut up watermelon to energize for a trek into the woods.

It is, of course, the season to gorge on watermelon and tomatoes—and blueberries and corn on the cob and peaches, until we are sick of them and welcome apples and squash and cabbage.

Full summer now slides into September. The angle of sunlight is shifting again. On some days, like this one, air blows up cool from the ground while our scalps still bead with sweat.

Chicory against the sky, Fawn Lake (DKB)

By afternoon, the bees have thrown off their weariness and the back-leg pollen baskets plump into tiny egg yolks. They zip around like heavily-caffeinated actors, investigate each flower briskly and fly off faster than I can focus my camera. As we hike after lunch, we gather our own nectar for winter: encounters with the plant and tree beings around us, and their own pointed shifts toward autumn.

Signs of autumn under our feet (DKB)

Thus that Friday also becomes known as:

The Day of Glorious Pink Joe-Pye Weed and Glowing Blue Chicory.

The Day of Burdock Opening Its Deep Purple Thistles.

The Day of Orange Slugs on Moss. The Day of White, Violet, Black, Brown, Orange, Yellow and Turquoise Fungus.

And The Day of Finding Variously Colored Aspen Leaves Every Few Feet.

Golden Leaves (CAF)

Back in April, I had mourned the coming of summer, the loss of bug-free walks and crunch of snow. Here in August, I mourn the coming of jackets and long underwear, the loss of flowers and bees and green-green lushness. However, the new season's gifts will reveal themselves: leaves that burn then drop, an opening of the view when trees slim to only trunks and limbs, crinkles of frost on chilly mornings.

Eventually I'll mourn the fall passing, then the winter, and next spring.

For now, the theatrical bees know their lines, how the plot develops—this is the falling action of the season. Autumn approaches with steady drumbeats toward the denouement. No wonder the aspen leaves, the changed light, this final frenzied putting up of nectar.

CAROLE'S MUSINGS ON THE COMING OF AUGUST

It's August, month of the Full Sturgeon Moon or the Green Corn Moon and the Perseid Meteor Shower. Here in the Northeast it's the season of small toads hopping all over in the yard and on the wooded paths, narrowly escaping the blades of lawn mowers and the boots of heavy footed hikers.

It's the time when the meadows are full of bees rolling in chicory blossoms, Queen Anne's Lace, and wild bergamot.

It's the days of garage sales, lush ripening fruits, flying grasshoppers, sticky mornings and cooler nights; the season when goldfinches wear their brightest yellow to sit on fences and visit matching sunflowers.

We have decided to hike to the Pickerel Ponds—home to heron, dragonflies and pickerel weed—and we arrive there just as the late summer heat is beginning to rise from the earth and yellowing grasses.

Although this is a magnificent morning, I can see that the time of brilliance is beginning to fade, shrink and die like the humpbacked gibbous, waning moon that sits in the mid-morning sky opposite the fat furnace of the sun. The earth is changing colors, and as I feel the dog days, and notice larkspur and water lilies in the ponds I see that time is not standing still.

In the bushes, chickadees are talking and whistling and I understand– or maybe only imagine—there is a message for us in the entirety of this splendorous dying, as if the spirits who reside here are briefing us.

As I stand looking at the water and musing this over, some grouse begin drumming in the forest, and rising from the woodland floor they sing:

Periwinkle wildflower (chicory) with green bee (DKB)

Periwinkle wildflowers
dying now
Drifting on the wind
a chickadee sings her winter song
Knowing I will also die
I listen.

THE CRIES
OF WILD THINGS

The hawk's clear, shrill whistle
split the wooded stillness.
Jolted, I didn't know
what it was that great mournful screech

but then the red tail flew from the trees
into open air
over golden fields.
Shrieking, she made a graceful flight
across the next meadow
into far-off forests.

Her screams stirred deep compassion in my heart
though if her cries were pain or joy, I still don't know.

The cries of wild things -
coyote yelps and howls
the *yikes* of the little frogs
as they jump into the ponds,
unmelodious crow caws,
peeps of hummingbird
add qualities of pleasure and poignancy
to this life of ours
if we but listen.

Pond frog (Northern Green Frog) (CAF)

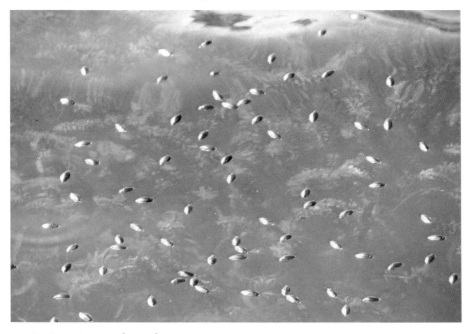

Whirligig beetles (DKB)

4 PONDS AND A BOG

One day a hiker came to kneel
by the bog,
bury her face in the muck,
inhale the mud,
feel the spirit of the stuff
from which she had been distilled.

She smelled the gathering fragrance
of congregating beings,
a scent elemental and familiar
the smell of family and tribe.

Are there dragons in the forest?
Or monsters in the ponds?
No,
only bugs kissing the waters for a drink.

The earth recognizes her, its child
as she dissolves into home
where bees hum the song of the universe … ….. OMMMM….
and dragonflies are angels.

And she asks that when she comes to the end of herself
when she lies down for the last time
like the dead frog lying in the road -
that it be on the peace of home
by 4 ponds and a bog.

The watcher at Wood Duck Pond (DKB)

THE STORY
OF THE WATCHER
AT WOOD DUCK POND

There we saw an older gentleman

sitting in a chair,

eating his lunch and watching,

just looking ….. and looking.

He might have been a Buddha,

he sat so still,

but there were no ducks

on the pond,

in the air, or on the shore.

He was gazing at the stumps, logs

and surface scum,

unbothered by mosquitoes,

deer flies

or gnats.

Froth on the water,
reeds growing by the edges,
stumps rotting in the lagoon,
and not a duck to be seen….didn't bother him.

I asked why he sat there.
He said *I watch for ducks*
and whatever else might come by,
maybe a heron, it doesn't matter.

He returned to sitting and looking.

We whispered good wishes for his day
and walked quietly onto the wood's path
where we saw butterflies and snake skins -
but still no ducks –
although I found myself also watching.

THE TRAIL
BY THE POND

This is such a holy place, this pond
and the orchard adjoining.
The ferns on the banks are browning for fall
and some are red and yellow.

Yesterday a blue heron fished here
though it flew off when I arrived
annoyed, I imagined, at my intrusion
upon its solitary feast.

Golden leaves against slate gray sky
shiver and then fly free in response
to a gentle breath that circles round them.
Birds whistle for You as the air turns cool
and You answer, calling them to their winter homes.

Maybe if I am very still
I will hear You passing by,
see You walking,
see the colors of Your coat,
feel Your heart.

Maybe – if I become like leaf or bird
I will know Your plan for me.

Frog from Vernal pond (CAF)

VERNAL PONDS

In the drying pond
the sleeping fairy shrimp
are dreaming water.

Dragonfly (CAF)

DRAGONFLY

Hey Dragonfly!
Where does that light come from on your iridescent wings?
I see no source of shining there
or is it within?

Long ago when you were dragon
and your fiery breath was warmth and light for a cold, dark world
I think you swallowed your own fire
and placed it in your wings
to warm and dazzle the air as you fly,
to make me bow in wonder
at your amazingly delicate flight.

Orange Hawkweed, ornamental but invasive (DKB)

THE GODDAMNED
M-F HILL

AT PARTRIDGE RUN, it doesn't take long for us to be challenged by the hills. The first time is the day of the fairytale woods.

That sunny morning we park at White Birch Lake and follow the turquoise blazes of the Long Path through woods and up a hill—"up, up, up a hill," Carole would add—to Fawn Lake and then Tubbs Pond beyond.

Along the way, we talk about writing and my upcoming yoga teacher training.

"I'm worried about trying to be perfect," I confess.

Carole thinks for a while. "You know that old maxim, Show don't tell? It applies not just to writing. As a teacher, don't follow a lesson to the letter. Say instead, 'I'm a yoga GUIDE.'"

I try to take this in. She continues, "A guide does it along with the class and learns as she goes. That way you can demonstrate how to be practicing instead of being an expert, instead of having to speak and do everything perfectly."

This reminds me of the Socratic method, to ask questions in order to figure things out. I don't say anything, but I start to wonder: How do I let go of effort? How do I experience each moment fully? How do I step out of self-judgment?

As I ponder silently, we climb the hill. An up-up-up hill.

Questions begin, this time out loud and from Carole. They increase in intensity and frustration as the hill circles up and around and along the ridge. "Will this never end? ... Um, why are we doing this?"

Summer path to the dock at Tubbs Pond (DKB)

As we steadily stride higher, I look down on broken trees that scatter the hillside below. I am finally feeling confident. "It's so pretty!"

Huffing and puffing, Carole stops to rub her hip. "Do you really think we can climb up this hill?" She stretches and twists in place. "Look at the rocks and trees. They got to just fall over the edge and lie there and not move again. That's what I want to do."

I don't know what to say. I didn't think she'd want to hear about experiencing every moment fully.

"Where is the top of this damned hill?" Carole persists.

"We are almost there," I offer. "It's a process, remember? We can take our time."

She harrumphs. "Easy for you to say. You're fifteen years younger."

I don't mention that idea of practicing she'd talked about earlier. I don't mention my old surgical aches either. She starts to move again.

We arrive at Fawn Lake soon after, and it is beautiful, and we forget the difficulty of the climb. We walk on to Tubbs ascending only small and gradual hills, and there are the fairytale woods to greet us once again.

Arrowhead plant and moth, in the water grasses of Fawn Lake (DKB)

The following winter, we hike out of woods filled with twelve inches of snow, onto Beaver Road. To complete our loop that day, we turn and behold with awe a monstrous hill curving straight up into the pines. This is our second hill challenge.

Carole's eyes get wide. "That's the biggest fucking hill in the history of the world."

We huff and puff in snowshoes this time. Hemlock needles blow down onto Carole's fuzzy red hat with its pom-pom. The scarf I hold against my frigid face steams my glasses. Carole slides backwards on the choppy surface,

Fawn Lake that day (DKB)

then I do. But when we look down, ferns fixed in the clear ice stop us. We pull out our cameras and gasp at the angled sun lighting up crystals in front of us. We kneel and take more photos.

Carole points to crackled ovals—air bubbles captured in glassy waves. "I love this damned ice!"

"Me, too. As my kids would say, this does NOT suck."

The wind kicks up. We shiver onward and up but grin as we do it. Then we have to stop and grimace and reset our pace, slower. How do we endure the pain? Is it worth it?

Panting, we reach the top of the straight-up hill. We are glad of our day and the sparkling black and white view over Partridge Run. We simultaneously hope for spring.

Spring and summer follow and lead to a warm September morning. We saunter lazily on the Partridge Run Road snowmobile path, which runs above a feeder stream for the Switz Kill. Evidence of Hurricane Irene from three years before still remains: parts of the path are torn away like a huge creature has bitten into it. Snapped trees in the stream tumble and pile like pick-up-sticks, accented with truck tires and boulders. We come out onto Kingfisher Road. Clumps of goldenrod grow so thick the smell nauseates; it's like honeysuckle with an overtone of decay. We can smell summer dying into fall once again.

That day our car is parked at a farther gate on Kingfisher Road. We could double back over the torn up bridge and through buggy woods and past Wood Duck Pond—or just walk the hot gravel road to complete the circle. The road seems shorter.

Soon Carole slows. "Will this never end?" I think she is joking.

Carole, behind me: "Why are we doing this?" I let her question sit.

"Do you really think we can climb up this hill?" In answer, I charge ahead with energy.

Finally out of breath, Carole stops to look ahead and rub her hip.

"Where is the top of this goddamned hill?"

I turn around to face her. A little wheezy myself, I try to be helpful, to be a guide like we'd talked about before, not a know-it-all. "We are almost there. See the curve? I think we go up and then down and around to the gate."

Wrong.

In fact, this is the worst hill of all. Every time we think we've reached the top, it drops down and then glides up again to the place we predict is the actual peak. But it isn't.

"This is not only a difficult hill, it's a trickster like Kokopelli or Coyote!" Carole mutters.

I agree. "No wonder we're cursing so much. But is there something to be learned from a trickster? Humility?"

Carole squints her eyes. "Maybe. But it's sly, and needs to be named. Hear that, trickster?" She shakes her fist at the hill, then gulps from her water bottle. "Trickster, trickster, trickster!"

We walk down and up again to yet another "top of the hill." It rises and rises from there with teaser drops and ledges we can't see beyond.

Now even I am frustrated. "I always thought that if I do the hard stuff, it's virtuous. Maybe even that good things will come to me because of my effort." I snap photos of bees on the odorous goldenrod and the twisty petaled ox-eye daisies next to them.

Carole shakes her head. "Often the trickster makes you think there is something to be learned, some benefit. This hill—it's what's in front of us." She sighs. "Shit is just shit, sometimes." She stops rubbing her hip. "I got some good pictures, anyway. Let's go. Go up this god-damned mother-fucking trickster of a hill!"

It actually takes us twice climbing up this road to learn, because we fall for the trick again a year later. Like childbirth, we forget the pain, especially since it looks like an easy walk when you ride down the road in a car, distracted by the flowers you might encounter on the way up.

We decide never to be fooled by the false promises of Kingfisher Road's "almost-there," never let the blooms lure us into thinking it will be all fun or even mostly fun. From then on we call it A Dishonest Hill and compare all others to it. Whenever we get tired going up a rise, one of us will repeat our hard-earned wisdom.

"This may be bad, but at least it's honest. It's not a goddamned mother-fucking dishonest hill, like Kingfisher!"

You can't see the half of it: approach to the scary Beaver Road hill (DKB)

Looks can be deceiving: top of Kingfisher Hill (DKB)

ODE TO A HILL

You are so beautiful,
adorned with flowers.
Trees lit from within
by a light
that is so holy
grow alongside your path.

You are exquisite
in your allure,
perfect in your display
of delight.
But I do not love you.
No I do not love you.

Hidden Pond, covered with golden tamarack needles (DKB)

THE JOURNEY BACK
FROM HIDDEN POND

CAROLE AND I had visited Hidden Pond before, but it's not a usual stopping place for us at Partridge Run. It is located far from our favorite sites, where the water sits higher than the path (hence it is "hidden"), and dozens of deer paths crisscross and confuse the often unmarked main trail. We usually meander in the milkweed for quite some time before finding our way. Uncertainty and wandering can be joyful, Carole reminds me.

This November day, she jumps out of her car. "It's just going to take five minutes, so I've got my hat and gloves, no bag." She also likes to travel light.

"Guess I'll leave mine too."

I like being prepared, but I'd already hauled my overfull backpack for ninety minutes down the dilapidated snowmobile bridge to Gifford Hollow. This would be just a quick photo opportunity.

"The laminated map is coming with me, though, since we got confused before. Do we follow the red snowmobile markers or the yellow ski trail signs?"

She shrugs. I tuck my camera in my jacket.

I try to mirror my hiking partner's nonchalance, but it's an effort. Each week she patiently hears me repeat the names of the roads and water features and how we are getting from one to another, even when they are familiar. I work hard to create maps in my head.

"Here's the meadow from last time."

Carole giggles at a familiar landmark: "Oh look, it's that penis plant."

"You said it's called mullein, right?"

Then there, over the rise, the stunning deep blue of sky reflects into still water: Hidden Pond ringed by tamaracks. The golden needles have fallen and made patterns in the water.

After we stand and listen to the quiet, then take photos and note the near-flooding of the path by new beaver activity, I refer to the map again.

"If we keep going, we'll circle around the pond and back to the road."

We walk on. The turn does not appear. We walk, and walk some more.

"What's that large body of water on our left? Hey, where are we?"

Once two winters before, we took a wrong turn on Beaver Road, and I didn't have my map with me. Carole was convinced we were going in the correct direction. We passed houses and farms and finally hit not the trail that we sought, but another road.

"Whoops!" she said. "But it's an adventure. I like finding my way. I'll eventually get to where I need to be."

"I hate feeling lost."

"But we know where we are now."

I will note that we had to slog up a really steep and icy hill that day, and she cursed the whole way.

In one of my favorite books, *Deep Survival*, Laurence Gonzales writes about becoming lost, that moment of realization when frightened people then run in all directions and become truly lost. Knowing this, I stand still in spite of my panic, in spite of losing Hidden Pond. I take a deep breath and look again at the map in my now trembly fingers.

I know we haven't headed toward Beaver Road where the farms are. No gate has appeared—or any other landmarks. Therefore, the unexpected water must be Becker Pond, the only large body of water anywhere near any possible path.

The give-away stream (DKB)

We have to be on the dotted trail that skirts Becker Pond, which we've only taken once before—when we'd come from the opposite direction.

That day years before, we'd given up on one poison-ivy-filled route and tried another to get to Becker Pond. We never made it. Exceedingly fresh bear scat in the path sent us running back the gravel track to the car. Our getaway vehicle had been parked at a pull-off next to a long couch dumped in the brush. Burned into our brains by adrenaline, the spot was forever after known as The Parking Area with the Abandoned Couch—even though the torn gray sofa was removed the following year.

I feel a little calmer now, reminded of that traditional memory technique: to note stories or experiences at a place in order to create a different kind of map in your head.

Examples jump into my brain from other days and walks. This is where the chipmunk popped out at us. This is where we stopped and took pictures of a feather in the ice. This is where the grouse surprised us with a thrumming dance. This is where we ran into the young man looking for a waterfall from his childhood.....This is where the bear scat was.

We'd had lots of those memory-building experiences, though not on this exact path or from this direction. Would it help anyway?

I look at my watch and squint at the winter white sky. It is 1:30. We have three hours of sunlight left.

In a way, I know we aren't truly lost. We might end up walking an extra hour or two; if incorrect, we could just backtrack to Hidden Pond, though now we are more than thirty minutes down the sodden route and prefer to keep going. I still take physical stock of our situation as if it is real danger. Which it feels like, somehow.

"It's not snowing or raining, and we are well hydrated and fed, since we already ate our tuna salad sandwiches. We have our apple crisp...damn, it's back at the car—along with the water."

"No worries," Carole says. "I love these hemlocks nodding overhead."

Hemlocks? I'm not able to look. My heart rate has moved into overdrive, and my feet are walking faster than I want them to. My visual focus has narrowed, just like Gonzales describes in his book. (I was wrong before; I was SO wrong. Can I get us back?)

The map seems to indicate we can keep going past Becker Pond, then a stream crosses over or under the path and soon after, an administrative/service road to the right. That road should take us to the former Abandoned Couch Parking Area and then High Point Road where our car is parked, though much further north. As we walk, I review the way out but also second-guess it. Ever since the map in my head hadn't matched the map in my hands, my equilibrium has gone tipsy-topsy.

"Is it the stream, that water heading toward the marsh that feeds Becker Pond? Yes, yes it is! Don't worry; the road should be coming up…"

No answer from behind me. Carole is busy listening to the blue jays screech at our intrusion.

"This is where we found the bear tracks. Well, maybe. I see gravel and rocks in the path like before. The service road is to the right. I'm sure of it."

No, no road to the right. Walk, walk, walk.

Carole, unruffled, "Look at the the semi-circles: horse hooves. And lots of horse poo. What a prolific animal!"

I realize I am hurrying ahead.

We come across a faint path on the right marked with pink ribbons. Carole's only comment? "That doesn't look like a road."

I know ribbons in the woods usually indicate something marked that is not obvious. It could be a way around an obstacle, or a trail disguised by the heavy overgrowth of summer and fall. A trail possibly known otherwise as an administrative road.

"I'll go by myself and see, but I think it's our way out." I worry that I am wrong even as I say it—will we be doomed to hike until dark, or worse?

Within a few steps, I know. From the brambles I holler: "Here's what we called the dark and mysterious stand of evergreens and there's the burned stump I thought was a bear."

Carole is not bothered by her misreading of the pink markers. "I knew we'd get out. Eventually." She grins. So do I.

There is yet another tall hill to climb, but the roadside is sprinkled deep with those golden tamarack needles. The sky is open. Thanksgiving is coming soon and we muse about menus.

"I'm making my Southern Chocolate Pie." My mouth waters as I say it. "It will be just three of us."

"We're having ten people over, and our pies will be pumpkin and apple."

"Look at the evergreen snag there on the right! That's the one we drove past last February." Snags are standing dead trees, and this one had exploded and splintered in that winter's extreme cold.

"That's the day we couldn't find any places to park, because snow had been plowed into all the parking areas."

More stories, more memory devices.

At the car, sipping water, I admit, "I have to go back and see where I made the mistake. I have to make the map right in my head."

When I retrace our steps, I realize that Hidden Pond is actually already on the dotted path to Becker, and that you have to turn around from the overlook and return on the original path. Or you will, as we did, be forced the long way around. It was supposed to be a five minute saunter to Hidden Pond, and it turned into an hour and fifteen minutes.

That makes me ask: Why do Carole and I get along so well as hiking partners?

Easy–we make decisions together. She actually respects my use of maps, and I rely on her confidence that we will be fine, no matter what. After all, we've survived ground bee attacks, impassable routes, exhausting hill climbs, hunters shooting a little too close, and getting lost. Together we walk and wander, have experiences and create memories—mental and emotional maps of our adventures—and now we have a new story to tell.

We go back the following week. The sky is even more blue, the trees almost stripped of needles, and thin ice has appeared. Hidden Pond is one of our favorites now.

Becker Pond (CAF)

MOUNTAIN LAKE
WITH CROWS

A lake on a mountain

open to the sky

... ...   (the lake has given calmness to the crater)

receiving what comes

rejecting nothing

... ...   (it is deep enough to hold all)

A feather falls in front

of the full moon

... ...   (a gift from the crows who call between the peaks)

Still waters receive its touch

and quiver

... ...   (a lover's touch on quiet skin)

Clouds touch earth

as she lies next to the face of spirit.

... ...   (in the mist, the lover's breath)

PROOF OF WIND

Bits of evergreen litter the winter forest floor.
White dunes of frozen drifted waves of snow,
like sand in an icy desert
greet her.
Her bones dance clumsily down the path,
Frigid air sneaks under her jacket.

She was hoping to see a bobcat
but no animals are up and about.
Not bobcat, not deer,
not bird, nor bear,
not even squirrel, fox, or beaver emerge.

Even the birds are quiet as if their songs have frozen.
Pond waves do not slap, nor lap the shore,
Yet, she says, *there is a presence here.*

Her breath is snatched by air that drops
from clouds
a whistling moaning, crying squeaking sound
Proof of wind
Proof of spirit.

White Pine needles on heavy snowpack (DKB)

JANUARY THAW

I AM STRUGGLING. And then I freeze.

First in September, October, and November come an extended burst of business activity, wherein I neglect much of my essay writing in favor of creative writing to build my new business venture. Stiffening commences.

A long viral illness runs concurrently. Painful anniversaries blow in; December holidays challenge. Whether it is the early darkness of the afternoon or the late darkness of the mornings, I sleep longer than I want to, resistant to pull up and out of heavy-blanketed winter slumber. Invisible, rime condenses on the edges of me.

The weather turns truly arctic; hikes become sporadic. Cookies call my name beseechingly, promising energy, and I answer, too often. (Those no good, sweet talking sweets.)

Movement slows to glacial, and the yoga attention wavers. Through this swirl of internal storms, I can't make out my wonderful new habits. Extra pounds creep onto my body.

I solidify.

Inside my hardened self, I start to worry: How can I get back to my contemplative life? Why don't I have enough energy to write about things that yes, really do, excite and feed me?

Finally, self-judgment crinkles the cold deep down into and over me like a winter lake, solid and thick. Mean-spirited questions follow.

What's wrong with me?

Will the blog I've kept for years join the thousands of "dead" blogs out there?

Am I a failure?

The tiniest of helicopter seeds (DKB)

Perhaps I freeze because over these months I would come home from hikes and instead of meditating on them, I would be planning yoga classes. Or writing about a workshop. Or processing how those classes and workshops succeeded—or didn't.

Corresponding with people. Building networks. Learning my new phone. Applying for tax IDs. Rediscovering aromatherapy, selling products locally.

-Ing, -ing, -ing. An autumn-into-winter shower of unique "-ing" shapes that softly, quietly, buries me.

Now it is January. We take a four hour tromp on the melting icy paths looping through the woods and around Tubbs Pond at Partridge Run.

Carole calls the weather a "January thaw." I've never experienced that at higher elevations before, just imagined it from books. Above freezing, the snow melts some and then some more and streams run.

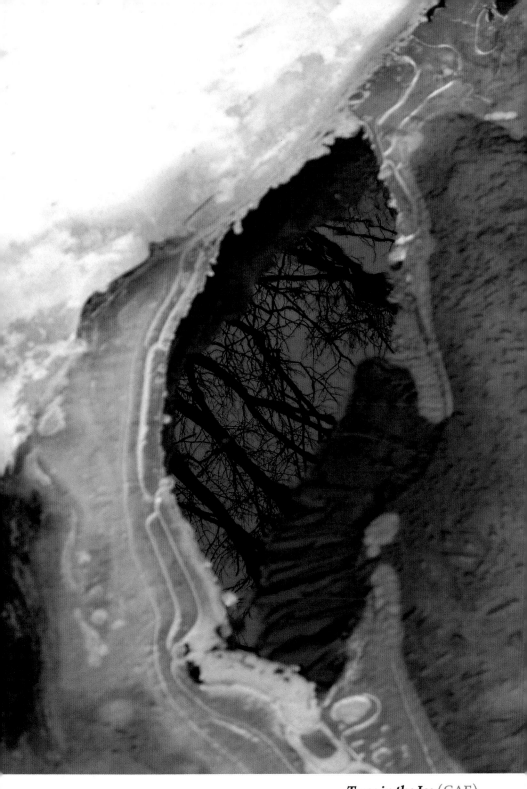

Trees in the Ice (CAF)

Fish in Ice (CAF)

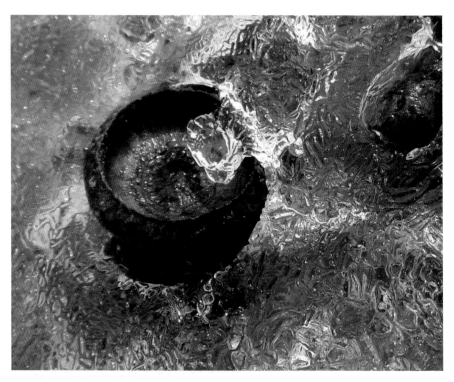

Acorn cap in the flow of ice (DKB)

Edges over Ice Crystals (DKB)

Winter milkweed at Hidden Pond (DKB)

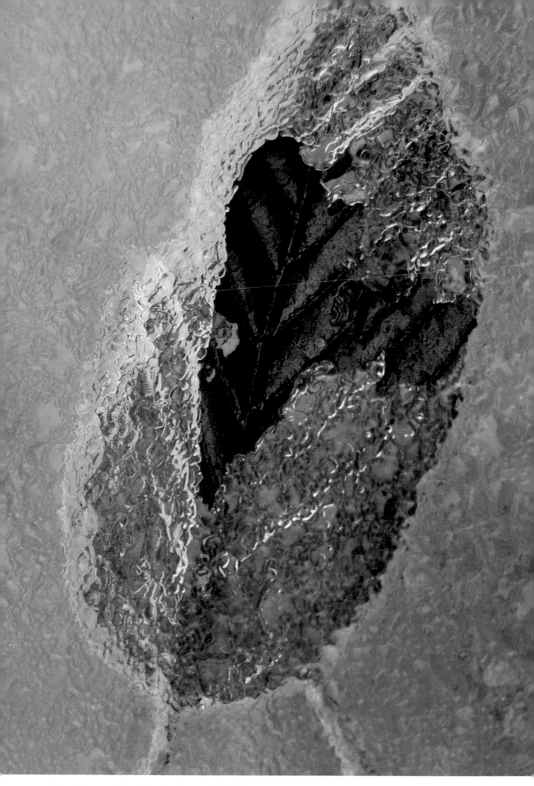

Leaf emerging in the thaw (DKB)

The legs are sluggish at first and don't want to pick themselves up over frozen upheaved beech leaves and stones covered by slushy moss. Carole's legs protest too.

We walk and walk, up and down. I start to sweat, pull off layers, walk and walk, get hungry, devour peanut butter and apples, walk and walk; I walk the worry out of my body, walk until I am so tired by dusk that my eyes can barely focus.

I get to see three ponds I'd not seen before.

And ice. Oh, the ice.

Photo after photo, I lose myself in the teeny tiny: a single leaf on snow and closer still the ridges of its veins; the iridescence of its decomposition backed by reflective crystals. Jagged shapes, clear, opaque, rectangles, rounded blobs, layer across layer of frozen, half-frozen, refrozen.

Miniature hemlock cones, red pine needles stacked over white pine needles, leaves trapped under bubbles.

We two photographers gasp, giggle, and gesture:

"Look here!"

"It can't get more amazing…"

"—Yes it can. C'mere!"

"I LOVE ICE."

"ME TOO."

The winter sun moves from white to gray across the sky. We stumble past Tubbs Pond and cheerily wave goodbye to snowmobile and deer tracks, and the chickadee couples who flirt as they flit from tree to tree.

My cheeks are ruddy, legs exhilarated. Days later, I still feel the warmth of following my instincts, listening to my body's craving for beauty—and the walking, walking, walking.

I think I've been thawed by the frozen.

Paper Birch wrapped in its shroud (DKB)

SURPRISES ON THE PATH

IT IS SMALL, strikingly bright in the winter sun, and rests on dried yellow grass not far from the pond. A rectangle of the softest gray and white fur shimmers in the January thaw wind. Belly up. All four pinkish paws poke out of its luxurious coat and curl up off the ground.

And where the head should be? First, a tiny red triangle of exposed throat.

Above the smooth connective tissue of the neck glistens a smaller-than-I-might-anticipate, slightly flat brain. No face, no black bead eyes, no whiskered nose.

Whoever slashed the little vole has sharp surgical tools. It was a quick move, irreversible, with no real struggle. Talons, we figure. An owl, red-tailed hawk, or raven interrupted at lunch-time. Probably by us.

I don't want to take a picture of it.

On past hikes we'd followed rabbit tracks out of the cover of the woods, where scuffle marks in the open snow were then followed on the cliff path by isolated splats of bright blood—the creature lifted high, bleeding in the grasp of a raptor. We'd also witnessed evidence of more obvious fights on a path from the winter meadow into the woods: a swath of fluff and blood and bits of intestine. Then drag marks.

I'd never used my camera or mentioned these incidents in my writing. It seemed macabre somehow. I didn't want to make it more or less than it was; perhaps I'd feel the need to editorialize and thereby risk trivializing—just because I'd captured the image. So I didn't.

But what we come upon this day is so anatomically precise, clear, and not savage or frightening. It is open like the vole's throat. It is clean, but not scarily. At least, I don't think so. I'm not sure.

What lives under the ice and snow of the marsh near Becker Pond (DKB)

I can always delete the photos later.

I am drawn in by the elegant structures exposed. Touched by the fragility of it. Aware of the anthropomorphic draw to fuzzy creatures, the Oh no! factor where we prefer the cute and baby-like to the musky terrifying bigger-than-us, of bears or cougars—but I don't experience that either.

I take three pictures. One angle: click. Move, another angle, click. The macro lens allows an even closer view, the final click. I feel odd: reflective, and yet detached. Maybe the photos will appear flat. Resembling a lab dissection. After all, I could make out bilateral glands at the base of what had been the neck and the thin intact membrane that wrapped the brain.

Maybe I would see it later as a horrific image—mammal with no face. Or voyeuristic. Too much like something a creepy abuser would enjoy, masturbating over someone else's pain. Or a bystander to something you are not supposed to see, somehow made normal—such as a fellow soldier separated into body parts by explosives.

But the portraits on my computer are plain. Sun on intact downy fur and what is gone and what is there. I feel merely the witness, to this after-death undevoured pose.

I don't have any nightmares that night, though I thought I might.

Viewing the pictures later, I think sometimes we feel like the little vole looks: laid bare, breakable. And also beautiful. Even in being torn open.

This vole says, "Here it is: the way we exist, live, die. It doesn't hurt too much right now—at all, actually—after the fact."

Winter sun over Pickerel Ponds (DKB)

THE POET IN THE WOODS

I PICTURE A POET.

In my mind I see her flowing, reddish-brown hair, loosely twisted into a bun to keep it from catching on low branches. She carries a notebook and pencil tucked into the pocket of her green-and-white-checked flannel jacket. Poet or not, she is making her way ahead of us up the side of the snowmobile path off the southernmost trailhead at Partridge Run in early December.

I know I am embellishing the facts with this mental picture—but in the woods I can clearly see evidence of her narrow, well-worn hiking boots. I can tell The Poet is short (because of her length of stride) and curious (wandering, then clearly stopping here and there), and in good enough shape to climb the side of the hill, though she isn't particularly skinny, looking at the depth of her steps. Snow fell the previous afternoon, so all the tracks are fresh.

Carole and I have ventured out on a sunny day into the glittering white of Partridge Run to follow the course of multiple snowmobiles along with plenty of hiker boot prints, dog tracks, square snowshoe indentations, and vole burrows.

After half an hour on the hemlock- and red oak-lined trail, we consult our map.

"Hey, if we bushwhack over the hill to our right, we can hit Partridge Run Road instead of slogging the long way around."

"Ok, I think I remember what the ledge looked like from the other side. Let's do it."

As we trek up into deeper snow, we are happy to see others have done this before us, including a large-booted hunter (more shotgun shells) and the woman I was calling The Poet. Due to the hunter's presence, I reimagine her outfit with a neon orange vest for safety.

Carole strikes out in front of me. "Look, she headed this direction, toward the fence. God, I love the old stone fences in the woods!"

Hip-high stacked rocks wiggle and waggle all over woods and mountains in the Northeast, often climbing up at near-impossible angles. In the overgrowth, other evidence exists of homesteads: rusted farm trucks, decrepit apple orchards, crumbled foundations, domestic roses gone rambling rogue.

An old sedan in the woods, not at Partridge Run but nearby (DKB)

"She went over here! Boy, her boots seem awful pointy for being in the snow! I wonder if she didn't know it was going to storm." The footwear pictured in my mind changes to western boots.

I follow one of the impractical Poet's side tracks as Carole veers left. The woman had scrambled over a tall pile of wiry brush. Why would she do that? If she were hiking over the hill like us, or even taking pictures or writing— none of those scenarios make sense with crawling.

My heart rate suddenly doubles.

"Umm, I don't think we are following a poet!"

Silence. Carole is obviously distracted.

"I mean, I don't think these are human prints."

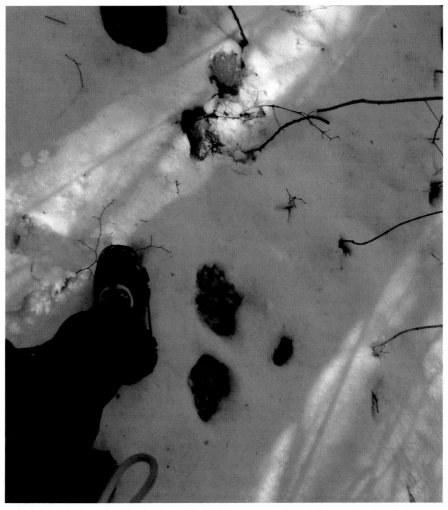

The tracks I saw (DKB)

"Huh?" She readies to climb over the wall to follow the recent steps.

As I hurry to catch up with Carole, following the prints between her and me, sunlight from the east glints in the rapidly icing holes. I can now see distinct indentations at the front, of claws, and then the somewhat loping pattern of full and partial marks stretched out in front of me.

"Oh my gosh, stop right there! I think, I think"—I can't get it out fast enough—"I think it's a bear!"

"What??!! Oh shit!"

"A small one. I think bear. If not, maybe wolf?"

We don't stop to pull out our laminated *Animal Tracks* brochure to confirm one way or the other.

Once again we hightail it out of the woods, sensitively aware how the energy changes when you believe you are close to an omnivore, even a probably-shy one. The tracks could not have been more than eight hours old. Maybe fresher.

The rest of the day we joke about the bear with a slightly nervous edge to our laughter.

"That bear was mighty tricky. Boots must have been uncomfortable on her paws."

"See those waffled rectangles on the side of the path? Tricky bear switched to snowshoes, just to fool us! Glad we are so smart…"

"Over here she's left shotgun shells behind."

"Can you see how she rode the back of a snowmobile, hanging off the side, breaking branches? How inconsiderate, that bear!" We move the splintered wood out of the way.

"And the beer cans up here on the side. And candy wrappers! What an ill-mannered bear!"

Carole, shaking her head in pretend exasperation: "That bear pretended to be a poet, just to get us up the hill."

I am glad we didn't actually stumble across The Poet.

Since she wasn't a poet at all.

WISH FOR TODAY

What I would really like to do today
is to crawl inside a milkweed pod,
re-emerge as translucent feathers
and fly gently on a wind drift,
or to sleep, sheltered in the pink budded bramble
of the wild roses
and later wake to a summer
of blooming loveliness
all around me,
or to roost in the twisted wild vines
next to a root-rutted road
amidst thickets of sumac
and fine needled white pines
while listening to the chickadees' winter song
sounding like God
whistling to his Heavenly Hounds.

BEAUTIFUL SOUL

Long ago the heart of God
like a cattail beside a pond or river
cracked and split
spreading life over all that was.

The womb of God
like a milkweed pod in the meadow
burst open
bursting followed by birthing
as silken spirits fell and grew
in fertile fields of creation
recreating love
and sprouts of joy
throughout the universe.

The sun discovered daffodils and sumac
as a Mourning Dove hunkered down
in the snow under a pine.
The icy snow that could destroy her is – for now –
her protector.
Her beautiful soul finds shelter within the breast
of the beast that threatens.
Isn't that the path of a fearless heart?

GHOST DEER

The ghosts of things given up
chase me through the woods and to the stream.
Was that a deer
or a memory
standing in the mist
watching and not departing?
Slowly the ghost fades into sunlight
and gathers again in cloudy skies.

Giving something up does not mean it goes away, it whispers.

So I honor its decision
and accept there are things
that circle around always.

Ghostly deer in the foggy pines.

Snowshoe prints, outlined with wind driven conifer needles (DKB)

ON AND OFF THE PATH

I'VE ALWAYS TAKEN PICTURES OF PATHS—forest, meadow, city sidewalk, even the sand next to the ocean's edge. Paths tell me so much about not only where I am headed, but where I am now, in which season and habitat. I explore above (light, trees, clouds), in front of me (pebbles, mud, tree flowers, feathers) and even where I've been with glances behind.

At Partridge Run, leaves, needles and acorns litter much of the ground, and Carole and I study their colors, how sparse or piled up, what the rain and snow have done to them. We also attend to how the earth reverberates under our feet, the sounds we make on gravel, rocks, uphill and downhill, even the difference when we're tired or energetic.

One day on a walk toward Pickerel Ponds, I am snapping shots of the hemlocks that arch over us while ahead sunlight breaks through shady woods at the water.

Appreciation bursts out of me. "I love this path! It's so beautiful!"

Carole thinks for a minute. "I like to walk off the path."

"But look at the winding trail! See how it leads us up into the birches? Besides, it's safer to stay on a path. It's like walking a labyrinth. You know you'll get there and back, and then you can enjoy the journey."

She pauses. "Why do you have to be safe?"

"I don't have to be; I just like to be. Today I feel a little stumbly and low energy, and I want to rejuvenate through walking the path, not having to think."

"Have you ever tried making your own way? You know, bushwhacking?" We reach the ponds, and she shades her eyes, watching for the resident heron that often hunts off a huge dead log in the cattails.

"Sure! Once, with a group. It was pretty tough. I managed to slip down the mountain and twist my ankle a little. Oh yes, another time, you might know about this one—almost followed a bear to its den."

Carole continues to watch for the Great blue heron without comment.

I feel the need to explain. "I know it's not always like that when you go off the path. I just want to get familiar with a place first, before I wander, to know how to get back to the path. I don't want to be stupid or put myself in danger unnecessarily." I further my argument: 'I don't want to stomp on protected plants, or wear a path where it's not wanted either."

"Well, I like to walk off the path," Carole insists.

I keep thinking about what she's said and feel my resistance. I know myself to be a rule follower, since that was the guiding force my first forty-five years. I still have a strong inclination toward it. However, I decide that day to pay attention to the pull of staying on the path and ask myself why I need to do this and entertain possibilities of not.

A year or two later, we'd explored all the ponds and creeks in Partridge Run and most of the paths. Walking back from Wood Duck Pond one early March morning along a slight ridge, Carole asks me, "What's that reflecting down there? Is it ice?"

I examine my laminated map. "There's no name on it, but it's here: a pond, a tiny one."

Carole says, "I am going to go to that unnamed pond next time!"

I am not too sure about the idea, but don't say anything. I go home and look at it on a computer map. I recognize a familiar nearby stand of evergreens on the satellite view and scrutinize its relationship to the mysterious muffin-shaped puddle of blue.

The next week I am determined to be adventurous like Carole. I share what I have researched.

"Since the trees are bare, we could go downhill from Kingfisher Road, and even though we'll be at a lower elevation, we'll probably still be able to see the road. I don't think we'll get lost. There doesn't seem to be much ice on the way down, and the ticks should be pretty inactive."

Buds encased in ice from running water (DKB)

"You worry too much. We'll be fine!"

Scrambling down, our cold noses take in the musk of decaying leaves. There is certainly no trail here. We slog through an uneven slough of ice and hillocks of grass. Sometimes my boots skid off the roots and sink into freshly melted water below the marsh plants. Sumac bushes poke us and snag our fleece jackets. When we finally stop to gaze at the frosted edge of the frozen pond, we hear only our breathing.

Then BAM! A crack of sound followed by a slow, loud echo—like an odd shotgun blast.

We jump at the sound, and then I reassure us (mostly myself) out loud.

"We've heard this before, at Wood Duck and at Hidden Pond, remember? It's a beaver traveling under the ice. I don't know if it thumps to warn us, or if the sound happens as they swim under the surface, but it sure is startling."

Carole smiles. "Someone knows we're here!"

We circle carefully around, ford a shallow stream feeding the pond, and notice an exposed opening to the old beaver lodge. Carole moves closer and takes pictures of the sticks and mud. I had tested my limits plenty that day.

"I'm good on photos. I'll just stay behind this large tree here and watch you."

Peering around the sturdy bark, I envision a disgruntled beaver leaping on Carole's back, biting her face while small ones tear into her ankles, and Carole breaking through thin ice to shatter her shin. Or dozens of ticks attracted to the heat of her body and the carbon dioxide she is panting out. Or an angled dead tree, a "widow-maker," finally falling over. Onto both of us.

In the midst of my exaggerated worries, I stay put behind the tree and don't say anything. Carole finishes her photos.

On each step back our legs break through the rapidly defrosting marsh grasses, up to our ankles and sometimes higher. I envision hours passing as we post-hole our way out. Instead, we puff up the rise toward Kingfisher Road. Brown and buff-colored leaves, heated in the early spring sun, fly up at us and make me sneeze. As we climb we notice blue plastic strips tied to the trees. We hadn't seen the strips before and realize that hunters had done this, so they wouldn't get lost when they went off the trail to follow deer paths to and past the pond, onward to the far off stand of evergreens.

Carole and I laugh, just a little smugly.

We didn't need colored ties. We had figured our own way to The Unnamed Pond—and back again.

A POND WITH NO NAME

A deep tureen
concealed by forest foliage
and therefore mysterious.

She was crafted by beavers,
quiet but for birds and insects
singing her secret name
and raindrops drumming her surface.

Dead wood and weeds clog her banks
where dragonflies are born
and live in her slimy gumbo.

To those who live there
she is the ocean,
that bottomless crater that holds the world.

But as this wondrous old bowl
reflects the clouds and stars
she dreams she is the sky.

I WALK THE LABYRINTH

I walked the labyrinth with your hand in my pocket
and your voice on my shoulder.
Your shoes walked with me.
We saw the barriers in life -
you can jump them sometimes if you want
but if you do you find yourself someplace
you were supposed to be earlier or later
but not now.

The smoothest way in or out is to follow the path
without leaping the stones,
until you reach the center
where the way of return is not what you think,
is unrecognizable, though it mirrors the way in.

Not following the path, I was lost in the maze until
I heard your voice say *Go this way with patience.*
What else is there to do, but follow the path to its end
where it begins again, notice what's in our way,
one foot, then the other,
breathing, opening, paying attention.

I said *I'm so happy to have you on this path with me,*
so glad you return when I call
and wistful when you go.

Tell me a truth, I said to you.
Tell me what you've learned over there after you finished your labyrinth.

Things just are you replied. *Just look and enjoy,*
there is nothing else to know.

Bleached tree in Pickerel Ponds (DKB)

Light through red pines along the Redbelly Trail (DKB)

TODAY I CAME LOOKING

Today I came to this woods looking for a poem

and this is what I found ....

In the distance, in the trees

a luminescent wave of foggy sunlight is piercing everything,

delivering the energy of Life,

the love of God.

A bird floats back and forth and becomes transparent –

a foggy lamination playing in white and yellow currents

riding on the exhalation

of the breath of God.

I won't hurry too quickly from this place.

I won't say *I'll be back tomorrow,*

For this light, this particular tantalizing light

is the face of Holiness.

Newborn Dragonfly (CAF)

LANDING: A TALE OF VERY LATE SPRING

In late May of 2016, I experience the first part of my Nature and Forest Therapy Guide training: seven cold but beautiful days in western Massachusetts woods, gardens, and farms.

Initially, I have a hard time settling in. I am distracted by calls from my regular life and then my A-Plus Student thoughts barge in.

I know enough to confess at the start, so in our opening circle I step forward.

"I don't feel like I've mentally landed here yet. One of my big challenges is to overcome perfectionism. Please help me make mistakes. I know life is about falling down and getting up, falling down and getting up, and I am still scared of both of those."

Later, one of my fellow trainees, Stana, writes on rocks for each of us. She gifts me with the message *Perfectly Imperfect.*

I land, and sink in.

One of the deep and unexpected pleasures of that week is to experience the outdoors like a little kid. I "break the rules" (whose rules? I ask now) when I take off my shoes and squish my toes into a huge patch of shiny green moss. Then I float my feet in the cold early spring water of a mountain stream. Doing that, I splatter sticky mud all over myself and then wipe now numb feet dry on my pants. On my *pants*!

I get amazed all over again by the shape of leaves, the sparkle of seeds flying, and the glow of dandelions in a meadow. I poke out my tongue to taste the wind.

I let myself touch trees and sit quietly for long periods of time.

When I return home, I feel full, maybe overfull—not just of natural connections, but also because I've met and quickly gotten to initiate deep conversations with almost twenty new people.

My apartment door opens onto piles of winter clothes to be packed away and a layer of dust on everything. The workload of the six-month certification process I've started multiplies then roils in my imagination like a thunderhead, and finally, a brand new part-time job starts, which will squeeze twenty hours a week out of what felt like an already constricted calendar. My thoughts turn dark.

Of course, life always changes and gives us experiences; some are simply a bit more intense. So I keep returning to that yoga mind to observe, ask what does it feel like? and not attach future-meaning to anything.

Landing back home is bumpier than landing in Massachusetts.

Luckily the forest—and Carole—call. We are weeks overdue for an outing. Partridge Run is our destination. "I wonder how the ponds are?" Carole asks, after a quick hug hello.

We start out on one path and run into the same damned poison ivy we'd seen the first time we'd spring-hiked it. We back out carefully, as if the reddening leaves might rear up and attack us, and choose another route.

We wander the edge of Hidden Pond where algae bubbles. Tiny azure flowers wink at us; bird's-eye speedwell (common field veronica) dots the grass along with dandelions.

I am busy with the flowers and what floats in late spring water, when she hollers, "Look! Look! A dragonfly! And I think it is brand new!" I walk over, and the creature is so recently emerged that it is still drying and unfolding.

The wings are like stained glass window panes but clear and bent-angled. They open to flatten as we watch, and we can see how the wings had folded into that tiny grasshopper-shaped exoskeleton. I'm no entomologist, but thanks to internet image collections, I've identified these brown casts—the exuviae—in my photos before.

I know to look for the white threads that until recently were attached to the digestive organs. Sure enough, just under our glorious new orange dragonfly, we spy its dry discarded shell. After taking many pictures, I move the grass back to partially cover the dragonfly; we don't want it eaten by predators because of us.

Right away I start surveying the pond edge. "I want to find one, too!"—but instead see a second exuviae. Then a third, and fourth.

Finally, dozens of exuviae are revealed but no live dragonfly.

"Our buddy seems to be a late bloomer," Carole comments.

I've been seeing dragonflies all morning along the ponds and paths and now realize where they had probably come from.

As I wander farther away from the initial discovery, I can't help smiling over the sloughed-off insect larvae skins and my inability to spot anything else.

Carole calls me over: "More! More!" She is practically jumping up and down.

In that moment, no chaotic apartment pulls at me, no fighting A-plus student worries about studies to come. I bound to her like I was five or eight, like myself. My pack thumps my back and swings back and forth as my excited legs pump me over.

—To ask, "What? Let me see!" To hear my pal thrill and laugh. To joyously kneel down and then slow my breathing. To see a smaller, multi-colored dragonfly uncurling wings, its slightly furry body moving in the novel light.

I didn't have to discover the sparkling insect. My friend did. I am now calling Carole "the dragonfly whisperer," to let go of my need to be the one in charge. I can experience and be grateful, let go of distractions and anxieties, and trust that all will be well.

I am starting to land again. As I do, let me be perfectly imperfect, a late bloomer.

Let me be an end-of-May dragonfly.

THE EARTH IS A STORY

Billions of beings
born from the mud
have returned to the dirt,
their stories and dreams
living in the skin of the planet.

Dramas, mysteries, comedies
dwell in the soil
waiting to be changed and used
for new growth, new stories.
Earth remembers each one.

Trees absorb the stories and grow on them.

Rising up anew from the ground
each generation
sings again the libretto
relives the questions
remembers the narrative.

The original, perennial crop of fables
calls to be born again
anecdotes to be retold, reused
until resolutions come
and they are free of the rebirth cycle.

These stories follow us about
as we sit by the creeks
and meander among the trees,
as we live our days
and drink our tea.

Life is not only My sagas
It is stories of all of Us -
as our lives intertwine
so do our accounts of it
and so it has always been.

The tales wait for an ear to hear
and a hand to write
so they may be understood, become legend
and be replaced by new accounts
so Earth can evolve to a higher story still.

Partridge Run Road, summer (DKB)

WALK INTO YOUR LIFE

THE JOURNEY STARTED out over eight years ago as an urge to explore nearby nature areas, familiar and unfamiliar, with a companion. After the initial invitation and its acceptance, we discovered ourselves to be not only fellow hikers and writers but also fellow photographers—and most importantly, deep friends.

We have walked our way through physical and emotional recoveries, through challenges we didn't imagine and challenges we did.

I have walked my way through first creating a new business and then into a day job to pay the bills—and out of perfectionism, workaholism, and a harsh voice with myself. Carole has delved into new art forms in ceramics, become a shamanic practitioner, faced aging parents, published two books of poetry and begun a new book based on her experiences growing up in Flint, Michigan.

As the months together turned into years and the photographs numbered into the thousands, we mused about how we are in the same place at the same time but often capture very different images. We also observe and write in different forms.

One day along the leafy path past White Birch Lake, Carole blurted out: "We need to make this a book!"

"Hmm, you know me, I feel a little hesitant," I answered. "What would it be like? Would it succeed to put our pictures and writing together?"

A few weeks later as we ambled in the shade, Carole brought it up again. "Have you thought about the book yet?"

As we discussed possible structure and themes, she joked, "You know, when we walk, we never get very far." More seriously, "Somehow that is important."

"You're right. Every time we are together, I rib you or you rib me, about how we take hours to walk only a mile or two." I knew it was because we can't help but stop and watch the wiggling, flying, crawling, blowing things, the trees overhead and the detritus in the road.

"Sometimes it's easier to put a book together if you have the title first," Carole encouraged. "How about *Walking a Hundred Miles at Partridge Run?*"

"Well, if we are going to do that, why not be ambitious? Let's get up to not just a hundred miles—how about five? Ha! That's outrageous!" I laughed and it felt good. "Five hundred miles, with our short walks!"

As we gathered and edited and (mostly I) fussed over the work, we kept walking.

When I tallied it up this year, I was a little amazed. Carole and I have walked about 420 miles together, not all at Partridge Run, of course—closer to our imagined far-away goal than I ever thought possible.

Our commitment starting back in 2012 and up to this pandemic summer of 2020 has reached 156 local hikes. That includes over fifty visits to the scene of this book, Partridge Run Wildlife Management Area in Berne, New York.

Eventually we will reach that arbitrary number of our title and then beyond it. We have other nature areas we've been frequenting and other books about them in our hopeful writer minds.

At this pace, I have further calculated, we expect to reach that first five hundred miles in 2021, give or take. Then it will be on to the next five hundred, or whatever offers itself to us.

We keep going, and paying attention, a few miles at a time.

STEPS AND LIFETIMES

a Prose Poem by Diane

A lifetime of beauty
life time in each walk
living and dying and the bridge between.
Green helicopters glow, browned seeds burst
sap drips, limbs fall
young hemlocks go crazy-haired
in white birch graveyards.

Walk the bridge
closer to the living
closer to the dying
connected to both
to everything
to each other.

Hear the first steps
in today's steps
snuggle next to Fawn Lake and its dam
or Newt Ponds' flood, or
vernal puddles full of frog eyes
stride your legs across the Long Path,
Kingfisher Road
into the trees.

Pause in the storybook woods.
Kneel, look down at all the
tiny universes in the leaves.
Lie belly-flopped on the dock,
touch the ocean
in Tubbs Pond.

Stop, close your eyes and listen.
Breathe.
Stop, arms out. Feel the breeze.
Stop. Then go, step into
the rest of your life.

PATHS

Do I care where this path leads?
No. It matters only
that I walk it.

Partridge Run Road, late winter (DKB)

ACKNOWLEDGMENTS

THANK YOU to the residents and government of New York State, especially the Department of Environmental Conservation, for preserving Partridge Run Wildlife Management Area and supporting our local Environmental Education Centers, along with other beautiful lands and waters.

Untold thanks to those who supported this manuscript from rough draft to final draft, including beta reading and fact checking: Ken Appleman, E.P. Beaumont, Madonna Behen, Cynthia Brackett-Vincent, Debra Burger, Cathy Callan, Lisa Hoyt, Annette Kavanaugh, Tina Lincer, Carol Tymann, Casey Mulligan Walsh and Mike Welch.

Thank you to our families, biological and chosen, for loving that we absolutely have to take the pictures and write the poems and essays.

Blessings on our writing and editing support groups and places as well: Diane's *Wednesday Writers Salon*, Pyramid Life Center's summer Women's Writing Retreat in the Adirondacks, Still Point Retreat Center, and our wonderful *Healing Through Memoir* groups, led by Debra Burger.

Diane Kavanaugh-Black (CAF)

Carole Fults (Debra Burger)

ABOUT THE AUTHORS

DIANE is a Nature and Forest Therapy Guide and in her non hiking and writing time works for a state agency and at a city library. Before moving to New York, her life included adult literacy work in Michigan, a massage therapy practice in Chicago, tutoring and teaching—and the parenting of two funny and wise, wonderfully huggable, now grown up humans.

She is busily at play taking more photographs and creating future books of memoir, nature essays and poetry; find some of it at *OfTheEssenceBlog.com* .

CAROLE creates ceramics and sculpts in wood when she's not communing with the snakes in her garden or the cows across the road. A shamanic practitioner and Reiki master, this year she has embarked on a master's degree in Indigenous Studies.

She is a gardener, a wanderer, a lover of being lost in the questions as well as the woods. Her previous books of poetry include *All the World Is An Asana* (2016) and *A Lineage of Dissimilars* (2020). She can be found at *www.CaroleFults.com* and on Facebook.

Partridge Run sign on County Route 6/Ravine Road (DKB)